How to Read Tarot Cards

A Holistic Framework for Your Tarot Practice

Lorne Caddick

How To Read Tarot Cards: A Holistic Framework for Your Tarot Practice by Lorne Caddick

ISBN: (Paperback) 978-1-7349673-0-2

ISBN: (Ebook) 978-1-7349673-3-3

CONTENTS

PREFACE

There is more to reality than the physical world. There is an energy, a spirit, a divinity that connects everything. This connectedness is part of all mystical systems, and it brings about a heighten state of awareness where insights and answers can be found.

To read Tarot requires the ability to connect with something beyond this physical world. Like all things mystical, how this connectedness is achieved is unique to each Reader. However, knowing that there exists a higher level of consciousness is the first step in the process.

A Tarot Reader also needs to have had a well lived life. Each card represents a life experience. The fuller a life, the more experiences. The more experiences, the more lessons learned and wisdom gained that is brought into the reading.

INTRODUCTION

Tarot reading is not just about focusing psychic abilities. It's a holistic approach that incorporates your life experiences through a framework that draws on other mystical systems.

One of the most important things I discovered is that there isn't one universal way to read the cards. There is only each Reader's individual approach. This is the way it must be because we are all unique. Everyone has their own experiences, their own psychic abilities, and their own way of thinking about things. Once I stopped trying to find the "Right Way," I was able to find "My Way," and everything fell into place.

HOW TO READ TAROT CARDS – A HOLISTIC FRAMEWORK FOR YOUR TAROT PRACTICE is a guide to becoming a Tarot card Reader. This book is about my way and is intended to get you on your own path. Think of this book as your starting point to developing your individual practice, not the finish line. The only Right Way is your Own Way built on your own life and your abilities.

FRAMEWORK

Pulling all the threads of a Reading together can be difficult for the beginner. To facilitate this process, I developed a framework that can minimize the need for memorization. It includes the selection of the Tarot deck, deck correspondences, card personalization, and the Tarot spread.

THE DECK

The Tarot deck should trigger understanding and facilitate the connection needed for the reading. If a deck doesn't speak to you, no matter how elegant the artistry, find one that does. I use the Rider-Waite Tarot deck. Arthur Waite was a member of the Hermetic Order of the Golden Dawn. I'm knowledgeable of the symbolism and it speaks to me. I refer to this deck throughout this book. Many Tarot decks are mapped to the Rider-Waite deck or their structure is similar enough where the information presented in this book can be converted to your deck.

THE CARDS AND THEIR CORRESPONDENCES

The Raider-Waite deck is organized by Minor Arcana, Court cards (type of Minor Arcana), and Major Arcana. This categorization facilitates card understanding. The Minor Arcana numbered cards (1-10) represent primary states of being, i.e., happy, sad, worried, excited. They can be triggering events, but they don't generally indicate a need for a choice or decision. Each numbered Minor Arcana card has four suits corresponding to an element that sets a context for their meaning: Sword (air) is intellect, Wand (fire) is transformation, Cup (water) is emotions, and Pentacles (earth) is manifestation. Therefore, Swords are concerned with things like planning, analysis, gathering resources, and problem solving. Wands are concerned with finding your true self, transforming, and finding meaning and purpose. Cups are concerned with relationships, emotions and feelings. Pentacles are concerned with manifesting (making things tangible or real) everything in life including wealth and health.

The Court cards (Kings, Queens, Knights, Pages, or the equivalent of these for your deck) can be thought of as the people or influences in your life. The Court cards, since they can represent people, are the only cards where I consider the orientation of the card - up or down. If down it can suggest a negative interpretation. If up it's positive. This is not a hard and fast rule, but it's something to consider. Court cards have a base energy which is the overall intention of the card and the energy of their suit (Swords, Wands, Cups, Pentacles). The base energy for the Kings is air, Queens is water, Knights is fire, and Pages is earth. Therefore, Air makes Kings the authority figure, Water makes Queens the caring advisor, Fire makes the Knights the drivers of action, and Earth makes the Pages the practical helpers for manifestation.

The Major Arcana are subjective states of being based on beliefs, needs, desires. They require some type of response, i.e., a decision or a choice. Each card has an energy assigned to it. Many of the Major Arcana are concerned with discovering the things that make you who you are—your individuality, your soul. The idea being that it is our destiny to "Know Thy Self" and to have the courage to live it.

TREE OF LIFE

I relate each card to its position on the Tree of Life to bring additional insight. I use this mapping when I present Card Meanings later in the book. The Tree of Life is a glyph (a diagram) that is used to explain how God created the universe and everything in it including you and me. It's composed of ten spheres and twenty-two interconnecting pathways between the spheres. Hermetic Tarot Readers overlay the Tarot cards onto the Tree of Life and use the correspondences for those positions to bring additional insight into the card. The Minor Arcana are assigned to the Spheres and the Major Arcana to the interconnecting pathways. See *Figure 1 Tree of Life*.

Other mystical systems can be used instead of the Tree of Life or in addition to it. The broader your knowledge of mystical systems the better the reading.

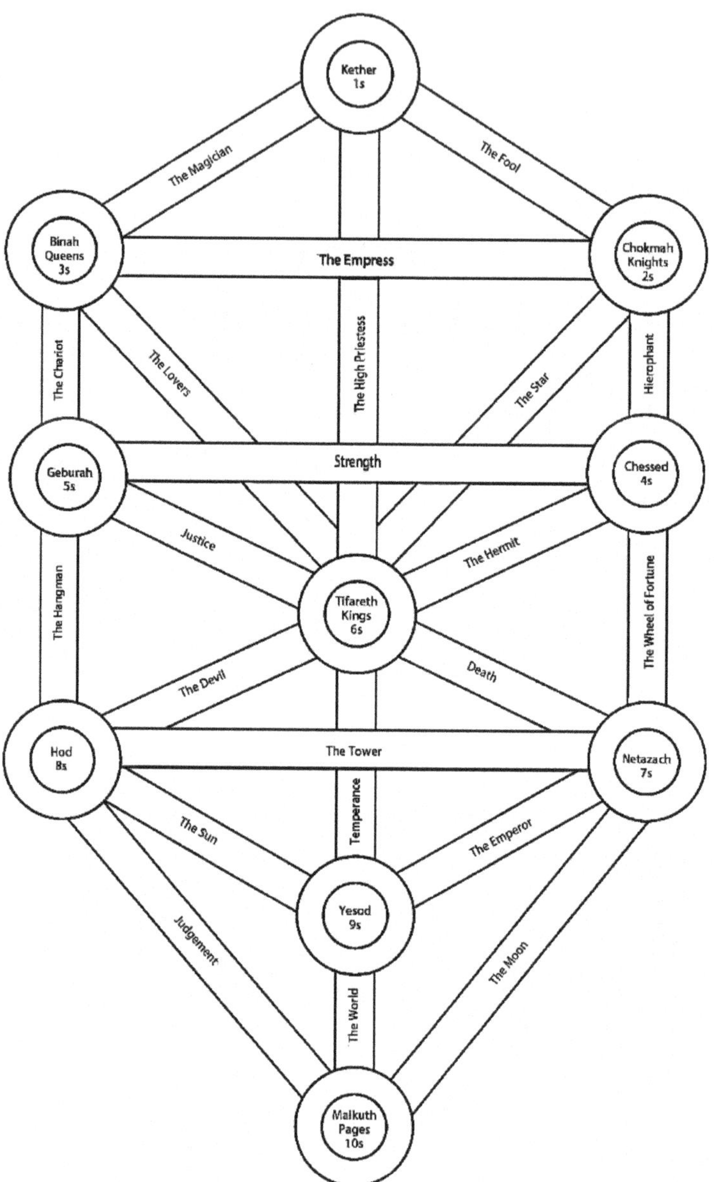

Figure 1 - Tree of Life

PERSONALIZING CARDS

A key to understanding the cards is to relate them to your life by personalizing them. What better way to do a reading than relating first hand to each card. In this way the Reader is able to draw upon their life experiences, lessons learned, and wisdom gained in the reading. Though the experiences are yours, the wisdom gained can be universal.

Therefore, when you research Tarot by studying what other Readers have written, understand that what you're seeing are their unique life experiences and practices. Take what resonates and leave the rest. Put together your own understanding. I don't think it's possible to be a Reader using other people's understanding of the cards.

SPREAD

The Spread is a pattern that the Tarot cards are placed on in order to conduct the reading. Each position in the Spread has a context for interpreting the card. Don't get too legalistic with Spread positions or card meanings. The role of the cards and the Spread are meant to assist in the Reading, not constraint it.

Find the Spread that works for you. I use the Celtic 10-card spread in Figure 2. In the Reading section, I will demonstrate the use of this Spread.

READING

A reading brings insights on the past, the present and the future ("What is to Come"). The "What is to Come" is for that moment in time. It can be changed if you want it to be.

I start a reading by going through my rituals to achieve the heightened awareness necessary for the reading. This includes laying out the cloth to place the cards on, clearing the deck by ridding it of any residual negativity, opening myself up to my deities and the universe, and infusing the deck with the energy I have collected.

You will develop your own rituals. Make sure they have meaning for you and signal that something special has begun. Don't try to impress anyone.

Once you place the cards in the pattern of the spread, let them speak to you. Look for the thread that ties past, present, and future together. Don't feel a need to explain everything, do your best to answer their questions. You will find that some people won't have a question and that's fine.

When I do a reading the first step is getting insight into what's going on. I then use this insight as the basis for answering any questions. If there isn't a question, I give them the "general" insight from the reading.

As you explain the reading some people will warm-up and start asking questions. Trust your abilities. Don't be afraid to be specific. Don't frighten them. Be constructive. Show them a path out if the "What is to Come" is dark.

What follows is an illustration of a reading using the Celtic spread. This illustration is intended to give you an idea of my method and how I understand the cards. Refer to *Figure 2 Celtic Method Based Spread* to follow along and refer to the card meanings in the Card Meaning section of the book.

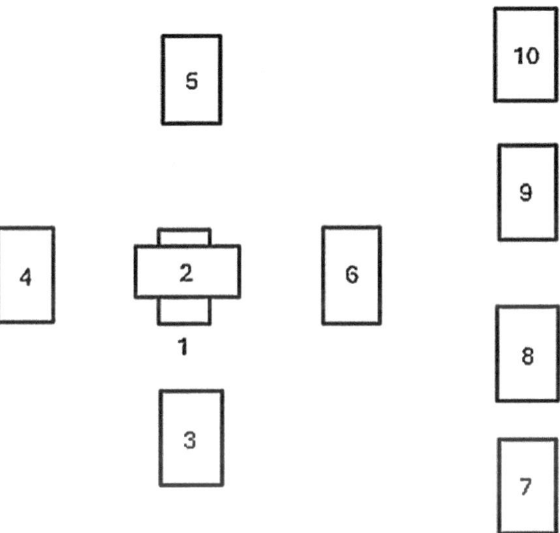

Figure 2- A Celtic Method Based Spread

1. Dominant influence at play
2. Nature of obstacles faced
3. Root cause of obstacle faced
4. Recent influences
5. Possible outcomes
6. Influences coming
7. The Querent's (person getting reading) influence on things
8. External Factors that affect things (help, hinder)
9. Hopes and fears
10. The final outcome – What will come

III

FIRST CARD IN THE SPREAD – THREE OF CUPS

(Three of Cups - page 47)

Spread Position

The #1 card position represents the current situation and the influences that are dominant at that moment in time.

Type of Card

Minor Arcana

Energy - Water

Emotions, feelings, and mood

Tree of Life Sphere – Binah (the mother, female energy)

The 3s are placed within the Sphere of Binah. All cards within Binah symbolize an aspect of birth. More broadly the birth of something new and the ultimate considerations. This can be an actual birth, but more likely it's the first notions and ideals of a beginning.

Symbolism

In this case the symbolism of the card clearly depicts joy and celebration which is consistent with the energy of the card.

Interpretation

The very beginning of something new is being celebrated. The energy of the card and its placement with Binah suggest a new or revitalized relationship is at hand.

XIII
DEATH.

SECOND CARD IN THE SPREAD – DEATH

(Death - page 75)

Spread Position

The #2 card position represents the nature of the obstacles faced that needs to be overcome. Also called the block.

Type of Card

Major Arcana

Energy - Water

Emotions, feelings, and mood

Tree of Life Pathway/Symbolism

In this case the symbolism depicts the death of the old in order to make way for the new. More specifically the message is that in order to move forward there are things that must be left behind.

Interpretation

In order to manifest the reason for the celebration of the Three of Cups, something needs to be let go. It's the thing that is being held onto that is holding back progress. Insight into what needs to be released can be determined in conjunction with the other cards in the reading.

VII

THIRD CARD IN THE SPREAD – SEVEN OF PENTACLES

(Seven of Pentacles - page 59)

Spread Position

The #3 card position represents the roots in the distance past for the block of the second card.

Type of Card

Minor Arcana

Energy - Earth

Manifesting tangible things

Tree of Life Sphere – Netazach (artistry in perfect balance)

All Minor Arcana cards within Netazach suffer from the distraction of Artistry in perfection. Too much of a good thing causes unintended consequences due to the resulting lack of focus.

Symbolism

In this case the symbolism of the card is not so apparent. A farmer is looking at his crop, which bears no fruit. The seven indicates that the crop has been in the field for quite a while. Fear sets in that all that hard work will not amount to anything.

Interpretation

Once before you've been in the situation of the Three of Cups. You got distracted, took your eye off the ball, and created an opportunity for someone to take what you've worked so hard for. Things worked out badly then, and you have deep scars from the experience. It's the "Once Bitten, Twice Shy" effect and it's making you reluctant to try again. But you must.

KNIGHT of WANDS.

FOURTH CARD IN THE SPREAD – KNIGHT OF WANDS

(Knight of Wands - page 45)

Spread Position

The #4 position represents the recent past. I tend to think of this card as the experience that leads to the situation of the first card in the spread.

Type of Card

The Court Card

Energy – Fire

Inspiration, transformation, meaning and purpose. This is a double fire energy card. Fire as the base energy and fire as the energy of the suit of Wands.

Tree of Life Sphere – (Chokmah, male force, action)

The Knights are all in the Sphere of Chokmah. The Knights contain the male force component of the Sphere and force action.

Symbolism

This card symbolizes the highest force of action. Its double fire energy brings inspiration and intense passion.

Interpretation

The Knight has forced you into action and that has brought about a situation to be celebrated as represented by the Three of Cups.

ACE of PENTACLES

FIFTH CARD IN THE SPREAD – ACE OF PENTACLES

(Ace of Pentacles - page 41)

Spread Positions

The #5 position represents "What's Possible," not necessarily what will come. This card takes on more significance after the last card ("What will Come") is played in the spread.

Type of Card

Minor Arcana

Energy - Earth

Manifesting tangible things

Tree of Life Sphere – (Kether, the beginning of everything)

It's the spark that ignites; it's the starter pistol that begins the race; it's pure potential.

Symbolism

This card symbolizes unbounded opportunity to manifest something new.

Interpretation

Something new is afoot and you have the opportunity to manifest the things you have wanted in life. This card brings life changing potential.

XVI
THE TOWER.

SIXTH CARD IN THE SPREAD – THE TOWER

(The Tower - page 77)

Spread Position

The #6 position represents the influences coming in the near future. I tend to think of this card as the direction which you are heading.

Type of Card

Major Arcana

Energy - Fire

Inspiration, transformation, meaning and purpose

Tree of Life Pathway/Symbolism

In this case the symbolism depicts a sudden end of a difficult era. The catalysts can be many—a death, a divorce, a job termination, a forced career change.

Interpretation

A sudden life changing event is near. It will require an evaluation of what got you here and the things that must be faced and changed. It's a time of soul searching and the discovery of your true self. It promises something better. This is the key to overcoming the block of the #2 card, Death.

VIII

SEVENTH CARD IN THE SPREAD – EIGHT OF CUPS

(Eight of Cups - page 61)

Spread Position

The #7 card represents how you views things and the influences you have on the situation.

Type of Card

Minor Arcana

Energy - Water

Emotions, feelings, and mood

Tree of Life Sphere – Hod (Making Ready)

It's the checking and regulating needed for final preparations. It's a tedious time for tying up loose ends and a time to prepare yourself.

Symbolism

This card symbolizes a state of emotional depletion and a need to put yourself first in order to recharge and be ready for what's to come.

Interpretation

You have been taking care of others for far too long and you have become emotionally depleted. To be of any good to yourself and others you need to refill your emotional cups. It's time to put yourself first so you are ready for the final push. This is a tough time for those that have relied on you for their wellbeing because they now need to fend for themselves. This is your time now, not theirs.

QUEEN of SWORDS.

EIGHTH CARD IN THE SPREAD – QUEEN OF SWORDS

(Queen of Swords - page 49)

Spread Position

The # 8 card represents your external environment and the extent to which the people around you help or hinder.

Type of Card

Court Card

Energy - Water and Air

Water as the base energy and air as the energy of the suit of Swords. Water: emotions, feeling, and mood. Air: energy planning, analysis, gathering resources, and problem solving.

Tree of Life Sphere – Binah (the mother, female energy)

This card is placed within the Sphere of Binah. All cards within Binah symbolize an aspect of birth and caring. The Queens specifically represent the caring aspect of the Sphere. They are the advisors.

Symbolism

The Queen of Swords helps you with making plans, gathering resources, problem solving and opening up your creativity.

Interpretation

The Queen of Swords indicates that you are in a supportive environment with positive influences. You have the advisors you need to figure things out and make plans.

IX

NINTH CARD IN THE SPREAD – NINE OF SWORDS

(Nine of Swords - page 63)

Spread Position

The #9 card represents your hopes and fears

Type of Card

Minor Arcana

Energy - Air

Planning, analysis, gathering resources, and problem solving

Tree of Life Sphere - Yesod (All is ready)

Preparations are complete and all is ready for delivery though maybe not what you wanted. There's no time left. It's time to finish this thing.

Symbolism

This card indicates that things didn't come out as planned and there's no time to make changes. The mind is unwilling to accept this reality and leads to a state of despair.

Interpretation

This card represents your Fears. The fear is that things aren't going to work out again and there's nothing that can be done. It doesn't mean this will happen. It's what you fear will happen.

XX
JUDGEMENT.

TENTH CARD IN THE SPREAD– JUDGEMENT

(Judgement - page 79)

Spread Position

The # 10 card represents "What is to Come."

Type of Card

Major Arcana

Energy - Fire

Inspiration, transformation, meaning and purpose

Tree of Life Pathway/Symbolism

This card depicts the start of a new era. A time to start over. To "Know Thy Self" and to have the courage to live it. Live life authentically.

Interpretation

A new phase of life will begin and with it a chance to know and be yourself. Others will see the change in you and some will be drawn to it. The opportunity of the Ace of Swords can be realized.

CARD MEANINGS

In this section I describe how I understand each card in a way that triggers me in the reading. These meanings, in conjunction with the card symbols, create images and sensations that allow me to retrieve the insights sought.

To aid you in relating to my personal triggers, I've included information from the Tree of Life to create the context for each card meaning. This is how I begin the process of personalizing each card with my life experiences.

The serious student should be able to use this information to begin the development of their own meanings and triggers.

Remember that the cards and their correspondences are meant to assist you in the reading, not constraint it. Good luck.

ACE of CUPS.

ACE of SWORDS.

ACE of WANDS.

ACE of PENTACLES.

THE TREE OF LIFE SPHERE INFLUENCES

1. KETHER

The beginning of everything new

It's the substance of all creation. It's the spark that ignites; it's the starter pistol that begins the race; it's pure potential. The opportunity it brings is reflected in the Aces and indicates that something new is afoot.

ACE OF CUPS
The opportunity to find love and build relationships.

ACE OF SWORDS
The opportunity to be creative and innovative.

ACE OF WANDS
The opportunity to be inspired and find meaning.

ACE OF PENTACLES
The opportunity to manifest what's desired.

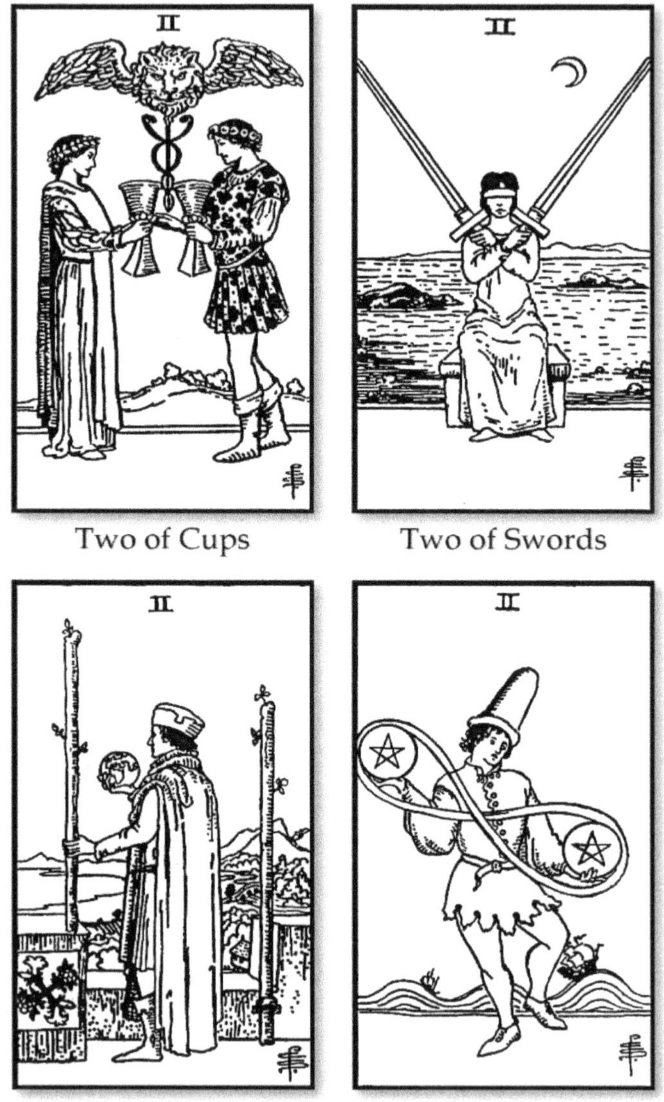

Two of Cups

Two of Swords

Two of Wands

Two of Pentacles

2. Chokmah

The father that is driven to create something lasting

It brings completion and wholeness as a starting point for creation. It provides a calm moment in time to figure things out before they get busy. It's a brief time of harmony.

Two of Cups

Finding Love and new relationships.

Two of Swords

Clarity of thought needed to solve problems and bring peace of mind.

Two of Wands –

The calm before the storm to figure-out life's path.

Two of Pentacles

The flexibility to adapt to change.

KNIGHT of CUPS.

KNIGHT of SWORDS.

KNIGHT of WANDS.

KNIGHT of PENTACLES.

THE KNIGHT

Knights are the force of Chokmah. They are a call for action and indicate it's time to move forward.

KNIGHT OF CUPS

Encouragement to enter relationships.

KNIGHT OF SWORDS

Clarity to know when it's time to put the pen down and act.

KNIGHT OF WANDS

Taking a leap-of-faith to chase the dream.

KNIGHT OF PENTACLES

Courage to take the risks that lead to success.

Three of Cups

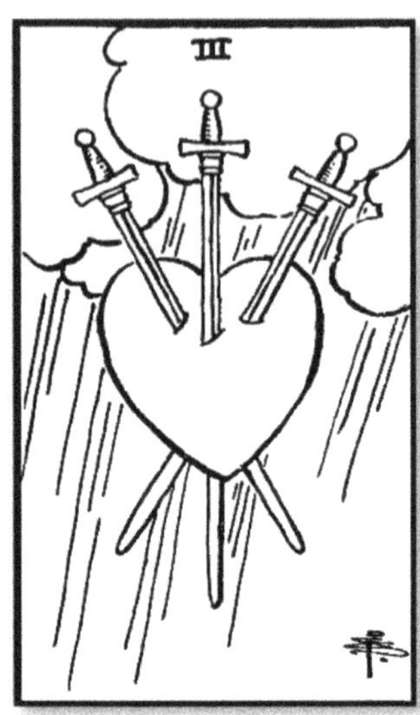

Three of Swords

Three of Wands

Three of Pentacles

3. BINAH

The mother that gives birth to ideas and desires

It's the first thoughts of what's wanted and an understanding of the ramifications. It's a time to consider how things will play out.

THREE OF CUPS

Joy and abundance spring from the new life created.

THREE OF SWORDS

Sorrow stems from the understanding that all births/beginnings end and the road is hard.

THREE OF WANDS

The infusion of integrity in all life's pursuits.

THREE OF PENTACLES

The recognition of good work to manifest what's begun.

QUEEN of CUPS.

QUEEN of SWORDS.

QUEEN of WANDS.

QUEEN of PENTACLES

THE QUEEN

The Queens are the force of Binah. They bring help and indicate that help is needed.

QUEEN OF CUPS

Advice in matters of love and relationships.

QUEEN OF SWORDS

Help in organizing thoughts and plans and obtaining resources.

QUEEN OF WANDS

Aid in the quest for meaning and purpose.

QUEEN OF PENTACLES

Assistance in matters of wealth and health and all things to be manifested.

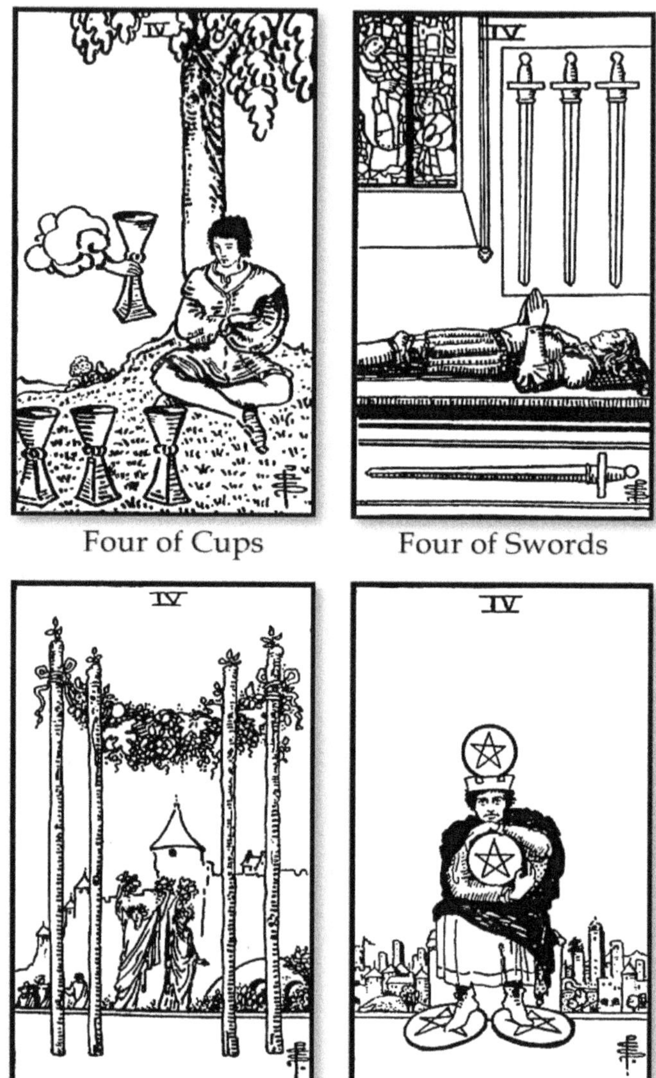

Four of Cups

Four of Swords

Four of Wands

Four of Pentacles

4. CHESSED

The first step where what's desired takes full form

It's a completion to knowing what's wanted and a start to getting what you end up with. Expectations and desires are set unrealistically high. It's a time of excess.

FOUR OF CUPS

The desire for more overshadows what is real and present.

FOUR OF SWORDS

Rest is needed for what is to come.

FOUR OF WANDS

Passions becomes unconstrained.

FOUR OF PENTACLES

Power and wealth are accumulated and held tightly.

Five of Cups

Five of Swords

Five of Wands

Five of Pentacles

5. GEBURAH

The Crucible

It assesses what's needed and makes the necessary adjustments to eliminate all that is unnecessary and does not serve. This signals a difficult time.

FIVE OF CUPS

Bitter disappointment when what was expected wasn't received.

FIVE OF SWORDS

Defeat when plans fall short.

FIVE OF WANDS

Strife when expectations must be lowered.

FIVE OF PENTACLES

Worry from perceived threats to power and wealth.

Six of Cups

Six of Swords

Six of Wands

Six of Pentacles

6. TIFARETH

The beauty of harmony and balance

It brings everything into balance. Life doesn't get much better than this—all is well.

SIX OF CUPS
All emotional needs are met.

SIX OF SWORDS
The peace of mind when plans come together.

SIX OF WANDS
A victory when purpose is confirmed.

SIX OF PENTACLES
The ability to be generous.

KING of WANDS

KING of SWORDS.

KING of CUPS.

KING of PENTACLES.

THE KING

Kings are the force of Tifareth. The Kings have the authority needed and are an indication that you need something from someone.

KING OF CUPS

Provides what's needed to complete relationships.

KING OF SWORDS

Approval to keep plans and project from stalling.

KING OF WANDS

Removal of barriers for inner pursuits to go forward.

KING OF PENTACLES

Approvals in employment and investment matters.

Seven of Cups

Seven of Swords

Seven of Wands

Seven of Pentacles

7. NETAZACH

The allure of artistry in perfection

It's too much of a good thing. The distraction from art in all its glory takes the focus off pressing matters. This is a period when things become confusing and focus is lost.

SEVEN OF CUPS

A downward spiral from too many desires to chase both real and imagined.

SEVEN OF SWORDS

Clouded thinking stymies results.

SEVEN OF WANDS

Challengers seize an opening and force a defense to your way of life.

SEVEN OF PENTACLES

Taking your eye off the ball jeopardizes what you've worked for and brings fear.

Eight of Cups

Eight of Swords

Eight of Wands

Eight of Pentacles

8. HOD

Making ready the final preparations

It's the checking and regulating needed for final preparations. It is a tedious time for tying up loose ends and a time to prepare yourself.

EIGHT OF CUPS

Time to put yourself first to replenish and recharge.

EIGHT OF SWORDS

The pressure to deliver becomes debilitating.

EIGHT OF WANDS

Swift action is needed to make ready and move out.

EIGHT OF PENTACLES

There's no time for mistakes (measure twice and cut once).

Nine of Cups

Nine of Swords

Nine of Wands

Nine of Pentacles

9. YESOD

All is ready

The molds are ready and the dies are cast. Preparations are complete and all is ready for delivery though not quite what you wanted. It's time to finish this thing.

NINE OF CUPS

There is joy in anticipation of the completion to come.

NINE OF SWORDS

Things are not coming together as planned and over thinking has led to poisoned thoughts.

NINE OF WANDS

The strength of inspiration is still present, but it's been weakened.

NINE OF PENTACLES

Wealth has been gained as has the good health to enjoy it.

Ten of Cups

Ten of Swords

Ten of Wands

Ten of Pentacles

10. MALKUTH

Manifestation

It's where all things become tangible. It's the kingdom of manifestation. This is where the rubber meets the road.

TEN OF CUPS

The joy of completion gives way to the trepidation of what comes next.

TEN OF SWORDS

Things didn't work out as planned leading to ruin. It's time to accept defeat.

TEN OF WANDS

The True Self was never found and its pursuit has become oppressive.

TEN OF PENTACLES

Wealth and health have been gained and all benefit.

PAGE of CUPS.

PAGE of SWORDS.

PAGE of WANDS.

PAGE of PENTACLES.

THE PAGE

The Page brings much needed practical aid. The Page is an indication that you need a friend to assists you.

PAGE OF CUPS

Assistance in bringing love and relationships into your life.

PAGE OF SWORDS

Assistance in putting plans and analysis into effect.

PAGE OF WANDS

Assistance in discovering your True Self and having the courage to live it.

PAGE OF PENTACLES

Encouragement in "pulling the trigger" on new ventures.

O
THE FOOL.

I
THE MAGICIAN.

III
THE EMPRESS.

V
THE HIEROPHANT

THE TREE OF LIFE PATHWAY INFLUENCES

1. THE FOOL (AIR) is a catalyst for creation.

It's a recognition that someone or something is needed. It drives a need for wholeness and the action to find it.

2. THE MAGICIAN (AIR) brings an understanding of things.

Important matters are at hand and a choice needs to be made. There's a compelling need to begin, but once the decision is made there will be no turning back.

3. THE EMPRESS (EARTH) is the door to manifestation.

The missing pieces are brought together and connections are made. Questions are answered and resources provided. Everything is made ready and it begins.

4. THE HIEROPHANT (EARTH) is living an authentic life

It's not just "Knowing Thy Self", it's living it. Living your life authentically and experiencing the satisfaction, the joy, relief, and fear that comes with it.

VII
THE CHARIOT.

VIII
STRENGTH.

X
WHEEL of FORTUNE.

XII
THE HANGED MAN.

5. THE CHARIOT (WATER) is the courage to hold fast.

It's the courage to hold onto your principles. They make you who you are, don't discard them for fleeting gain or the approval of others.

6. STRENGTH (FIRE) is making your own way.

It's having the confidence, willpower and strength to control your life. Accept your faults and don't look for others to blame.

7. THE WHEEL OF FORTUNE (FIRE) drives a need for change.

It's a quest for something that might not be clearly known or even exist. The status quo is intolerable and the stalemate must be broken.

8. THE HANGED MAN (WATER) is a sacrifice to redeem oneself.

It's giving up something of value to mend or improve a relationship. Acting shamefully requires a sacrifice to put things right.

II
B
J
THE HIGH PRIESTESS

XVII
THE STAR.

VI
THE LOVERS.

IX
THE HERMIT.

9. THE HIGH PRIESTESS (WATER) is a rediscovery of your best self

It's raising above life's daily struggles by the incorporation of your highest principles in everything you do.

10. THE STAR (FIRE) is the true path that illuminates the inner self

It shows the path forward and requires will and determination to stay the course.

11. THE LOVERS (AIR) is taking a risk in a relationship for a chance of something better

It's making a choice with the hope of improving the union. It's an assessment that will require faith and sacrifice to follow a new destiny.

12. THE HERMIT (EARTH) is the figuring out of how to manifest what's desired

It's knowing yourself, your talents, and the things available to you in order to manifest what you need and want.

XI
JUSTICE.

XIII
DEATH.

XIV
TEMPERANCE.

XV
THE DEVIL.

13. JUSTICE (AIR) is making things right

It's the ability to face up to faults, accept responsibility, and do what's needed to restart.

14. DEATH (WATER) is to let the past die in order to be born anew

It's a willingness to let go and face an unknown future for the hope of something better.

15. TEMPERANCE (FIRE) is finishing what you started

It's a strengthening and confirming process that results in standing on your own two feet spiritually and physically.

16. THE DEVIL (EARTH) is confronting and conquering evil

It's acknowledging evil, facing it, and riding yourself of it through good purpose.

IV
THE EMPEROR.

XVI
THE TOWER.

XIX
THE SUN .

THE MOON.

17. THE EMPEROR (AIR) is the stable environment that is necessary for creativity in all pursuits

It's having everything necessary to drive solutions. It's all up to you now, no one else. Take control.

18. THE TOWER (FIRE) is the end of an era

It's an abrupt difficult ending to a phase of life. It heralds the coming of something new and unknown. It promises an emancipation of the spirit.

19. THE SUN (FIRE) is freedom

It's blue skies and clear sailing. The restrictions of the past are gone and adjustments have been made. A great enlightenment has occurred.

20. THE MOON (WATER) is facing the fears that have dominated

It's time to face the fears that have held you back. It's a dark time, but the promise of a new dawn and the bright warm days of summer lay ahead.

XX
JUDGEMENT.

XXI
THE WORLD.

21. JUDGEMENT (FIRE) is the start of a new era

It brings an awaking to new and higher levels of thought and another chance to live out principles held dear and begin a new life.

22. THE WORLD (EARTH) is an ending to a cycle.

It's a time for introspection on experiences had, lessons learned, and wisdom gained. Take comfort in the completion and anticipate the new beginning.

CONCLUSION

It can be difficult to read Tarot unless your psychic abilities are so strong that you just use the card directly as a trigger. Unfortunately, most of us will need something more. Don't fret, you're in good company, which includes me.

With each reading you'll get better. Keep learning. Meditate on the cards and think about how they speak to you. If you stick with it, there will be a moment when you'll get it. You will have arrived. Also, continue to experience new things. The lessons learned will serve you well in life and Tarot.

www.ingramcontent.com/pod-product-compliance
Ingram Content Group UK Ltd.
Pitfield, Milton Keynes, MK11 3LW, UK
UKHW062308290726
14090UKWH00018B/946